IRELAND

IRELAND

PORTRAYED BY GORDON WETMORE

FOREWORD BY PRINCESS GRACE OF MONACO

THOMAS NELSON PUBLISHERS
Nashville

ACKNOWLEDGMENTS

Selection of the literary quotations in *Ireland* was made by George Wieser.

The excerpt on page 12 from *The Irish Mystique* by Max Caulfield, copyright 1973 by Max Caulfield, is reprinted by permission of Prentice-Hall, Inc., Englewood Cliffs, New Jersey.

The excerpt on page 36 from *I Knock at the Door* by Sean O'Casey is reprinted by permission of St. Martin's Press, Inc., New York, New York, and Macmillan & Co., Ltd., London, England.

A portion of the poem "The Coolin" on page 39 from *Collected Poems* by James Stephen, copyright 1918 by Macmillan Publishing Co., Inc., renewed 1946 by James Stephens, is reprinted with permission of Macmillan Publishing Co., Inc., New York, New York, and The Macmillan Company of Canada Ltd., and Macmillan Press Ltd.

The excerpt on pages 42 and 43 from *Ghost Stories* by Shane Leslie is reprinted with permission of The Bodley Head, London, England.

A portion of the poem "Dublin" by Louis MacNeice on page 48 is reprinted by permission of Faber and Faber Ltd., London, England, from *The Collected Poems of Louis MacNeice.*

Portions of the poems "The Stolen Child" on page 51 and "The Lake Isle of Innisfree" on page 53 from *Collected Poems* by William Butler Yeats, copyright © 1906 by Macmillan Publishing Co., Inc., renewed 1934 by William Butler Yeats, are reprinted by permission of Macmillan Publishing Co., Inc., New York, New York, and A. P. Watt Ltd., London, England.

Grateful acknowledgement is given to Thornton Cox Publishers, London, England, for permission to quote from *Travellers' Guide to Ireland* on pages 56 and 124.

The excerpts from "A Landlord's Garden in County Wicklow" on page 59 and "The Aran Islands" on pages 115 and 119 taken from *The Aran Islands and Other Writings* by John Millington Synge are reprinted by permission of Random House, Inc., New York, New York, and Allen S. Unwin, Ltd., London, England.

The excerpt on page 63 from *As I Was Going Down Sackville Street* by Oliver St. John Gogarty is reprinted by permission of Harcourt Brace Jovanovich, Inc., New York, New York, and Olive Duane Gogarty, Dublin, Ireland.

The excerpt on page 65 from *The Irish Republic* by Dorothy Macardle, copyright © 1965 by Keirleach De Valera, is reprinted by permission of the Lincoln Educational Foundation, Inc., New York, New York.

The excerpts on pages 66 and 104 from *A Literary Guide to Ireland* by Thomas Cahill and Susan Cahill, copyright © 1973 by Thomas Cahill and Susan Cahill, are reprinted by permission of Charles Scribner's Sons, New York, New York.

The excerpt on page 69 from "When the Moon Has Set" by John Millington Synge is reprinted by permission of Random House, New York, New York.

The poem "Sunday in Ireland" by John Betjeman on page 75 is reprinted from *Collected Poems* by permission of John Murray (Publishers) Ltd., London, England, and Houghton Mifflin Co., Boston, Massachusetts.

The poem "The Workman's Friend" on page 85 from *At Swim Two Birds* by Flann O'Brien, © 1966 by Brian Nolan, is reprinted by permission of Walker and Company, Inc., New York, New York.

A portion of the poem "Meditations in Time of Civil War" on page 88 from *Collected Poems* by William Butler Yeats, copyright © 1928 by Macmillan Publishing Co., Inc., renewed 1956 by Georgie Yeats, is reprinted by permission of Macmillan, New York, New York, and A. P. Watt Ltd., London, England.

The excerpt on page 91 from *Bowen's Court,* Second Edition, by Elizabeth Bowen is reprinted by permission of Random House, New York, New York, and Curtis Brown Ltd., New York, New York.

The excerpt on page 107 from "The Dead" in *Dubliners* by James Joyce, copyright © 1967 by the Estate of James Joyce, is reprinted by permission of Viking Penguin Inc., New York, New York, and The Society of Authors, London, England.

The excerpt on page 127 from *Portrait of an Artist as a Young Man* by James Joyce, copyright © 1916 by B. W. Huebsch, © 1944 by Nora Joyce, is reprinted by permission of Viking Penguin Inc., New York, New York, and The Society of Authors, London, England.

Copyright © 1980 by Gordon Wetmore

Library of Congress Cataloging in Publication Data
  Wetmore, Gordon.
    Ireland.
    1. Wetmore, Gordon. 2. Ireland in art. 3. Ireland—Description and travel—1951-   I. Title.
  ND237.W56A4   1980   759.13   80-18913
    ISBN 0-8407-4085-9

Book design by Nancy Bozeman

CONTENTS

FOREWORD

My pleasure in viewing the work of Gordon Wetmore in this magnificent book was, no doubt, greatly influenced by my love for the country of my paternal grandparents, John Henry Kelly and Mary Costello Kelly. They came to the United States from County Mayo, Ireland, as youngsters. They were people of remarkable character. I see that kind of character etched in the faces of these indomitable people in Gordon Wetmore's work. In this lovely book artist Wetmore has captured the gentleness and beauty of everyday life.

The essence of Ireland—the splendor of its emerald beauty, the rugged men who still labor with horsedrawn carts, the thatched-roofed cottages, the darling children—is here in *Ireland, Portrayed by Gordon Wetmore.* I shall return often to the pages of this charming book.

Grace de Monaco

Grace of Monaco

IRELAND
THE EMERALD ISLE

A few years ago when I collaborated with Leon Uris on *Promised Land* —a book containing my paintings of Israel—he told me of the similarities between the Jewish and Irish peoples. Both have struggled to maintain their identity. Both Israel and Ireland have a population of a bit more than four million people and live with the constant reality of terrorism. Both countries have experienced a dispersal of their people throughout the world, and yet the Irish and the Jewish peoples have maintained an attachment to their forefathers and an intense love of their homelands. Both American Jews and the American Irish have been important influences in the politics of their respective lands, for there are more people of Irish descent in America than in Ireland, just as there are more Jews in New York City than in Tel Aviv and Jerusalem combined. The parallels could go on and on.

But when I went to Ireland, I found that for all the similarities between the Jewish and Irish peoples, the differences between the two countries are striking. In Israel it is far too easy to be caught up in the *places* there— the shrines, the relics, the buildings, the sites, the places where Abraham and David and Solomon and Jesus lived—and to overlook the *people.* In fact, although Israel is a Jewish state, it has a heterogenous population made up of Jews and Moslems and Christians, each group maintaining its own identity. Ireland, however, has tended to conquer its conquerors, causing them to become more Irish than the Irish. This was demonstrated by the famous statutes of Kilkenny, passed in 1367, which forbade the English settlers from having any association with the Irish because they had stopped speaking English and had adopted Irish ways. "Irishness" characterizes all inhabitants of the Emerald Isle: Catholics and Protestants, land-holders, and tinkers, established families and recent immigrants. The population is more homogeneous than that of Israel.

Moreover, Ireland has few sites and relics as famous as Israel's. Admittedly, there are more than three thousand castles in Ireland, and an island in Lough Derg where St. Patrick is said to have fasted for forty days, and the Custom House in Dublin, and the Book of Kells in Trinity College— but what is important is the Irish people. One is usually drawn to Israel to *see places;* one should not leave Ireland without getting to *know people.* This is reflected in this book by the number of paintings of people—people I saw, met, and came to know in Ireland. I went to the pubs, the churches, and the guest houses, and I made friends. I feel as if I *visited* Israel, but *lived in* Ireland. This book is a portrait not just of a land, but of a people and the way they live.

The Irish Mystique

We Americans have a strong identification with Ireland, for the Irish immigrant and his descendants have played an important role in our history. We have a folk hero in the traditional Irish policeman in Boston or New York. John Sullivan, James Corbett, Jack Dempsey, and Gene Tunney were all Irish boxing champions. The Irish have played a dominant role in the Catholic church in America and have given us Fordham and Notre

WOMAN IN FARMYARD/*County Tipperary*

11

Dame universities. The Democratic party has been heavily represented with Irishmen: Mayor Daley, Honey Fitz, Patrick Moynihan, Eugene McCarthy, and of course the Kennedys. In fact, on the day John Kennedy died, the president of the United States, the speaker of the House of Representatives, and the majority leader of the Senate were all Irish, all Catholics, and all Democrats. And America probably celebrates St. Patrick's Day with more vigor than any other country in the world: The Chicago River is dyed green, New York paints an emerald line down Fifth Avenue, supermarket ads are filled with shamrocks and leprechauns, and everyone claims an Irish heritage—if only for a day.

But when I went to Ireland I discovered that for the most part the Irish are very different from any stereotype. The real Ireland has a charm—a mystique—that captures the visitor. This mystique includes the honesty of the people, their concern for the development of the human spirit rather than a political empire, the tragic fight for freedom and identity that has been their history, and their identification with their Celtic past and medieval glories. It includes nostalgia, as Irish writer Sean O'Faolain suggests:

I suppose why people are interested in us today is that they have this idea that Ireland's a lovely old place, with quaint, lazy ways, and that we're indestructible; that we'll never change. I'd say it was all nostalgia. . . .

The Americans have destroyed their own country, the English are busy ruining theirs, and the Germans and other continentals are going mad, locked up in bursting cities with motor cars everywhere and the threat of The Bomb or something awful like that constantly hanging over them. I often see them out there on the west coast, standing on a bit of rock and getting salt-sprayed from the rollers, and you can almost hear them say, "Isn't this really lovely?" It's the tranquility of it all. . . .

But that's our trouble, you know. The things that have kept Ireland as she is—the old folk values, in other words—will no longer work in the modern world. And that puts us in a dilemma. Today we're absolutely torn between wanting to produce fellows with cold, clear, rational-type minds and a people who value the old, easygoing, delightful society—a people who believe leisure and companionship are more important than "success"— whatever that is—or money. What we're really talking about, I suppose, is not *what* the Irish mystique adds up to—but is it going to last?[1]

When I think of Ireland, I remember the silent, slow-motion flame of a peat fire and long walks with my wife Connie in the evenings on narrow lanes threading through farmlands. The Irish mystique is not merely nostalgia, but a way of life which, according to some Irish, takes an Englishman three days to adjust to and an American two weeks. Inconvenience and interruptions seem to be taken in stride. When a bank strike was threatened and we anxiously tried to withdraw our money, the teller advised, "Ahh, I wouldn't do that, because then again, they may *not* strike, you know."

It is this way of life, this charm, this mystique that I have tried to capture.

1. MAX CAULFIELD, *The Irish Mystique* (Englewood Cliffs, N.J.: Prentice Hall, 1973), p. 7.

To talk of the Blarney Stone, Shannon airport's duty-free shops, or other guidebook features is interesting but not essential to portraying the Ireland I saw: A country with pure, delicious water and clear, fresh-smelling air, a country with its heritage still intact, a country with a balanced way of living which is, unfortunately, fragile in our modern world.

A Brief History

Although Ireland was inhabited more than three thousand years ago, the first group of people to have left a lasting impression was the Celts, who arrived about 350 B.C. In the first century B.C., Diodorus Siculus, a Greek historian, described the Celts as physically "terrifying in appearance, with deep-sounding and very harsh voices. In conversation they use few words and speak in riddles, for the most part hinting at things and leaving a great deal to be understood. They frequently exaggerate with the aim of extolling themselves and diminishing the status of others. They are boasters and threateners and given to bombastic self-dramatization, and yet they are quick of mind and with good natural ability for learning. They have also lyric poets whom they call Bards. They sing to the accompaniment of instruments resembling lyres."

The Celts introduced the plough, built hillforts, and were skilled in metalcraft and weaving. Their religious leaders were the druid priests, who also acted as judges and teachers. The Celts gave the island its name, which today is known in Gaelic as "Eire." Although the Roman Empire spread its unifying and civilizing influence over most of Europe and Great Britain, it never crossed the short distance to Irish shores, and thus Ireland was able to retain a pure Celtic heritage.

The Irish Celts were fierce invaders of neighboring lands, and on one such expedition in about A.D. 400 they kidnapped a boy—probably in England—named Patrick who was sold into slavery and forced to herd swine for six years in Ireland. At the end of that time Patrick escaped and made his way back to his family. After his conversion to Christianity and ordination to the priesthood, he was guided by a vision to return to Ireland as a missionary. Patrick's influence transformed Ireland into a land of saints and scholars. The church that developed in Ireland was centered around monasteries, and in the Dark Ages Ireland was known as the center of learning. Whereas the Celtic culture had been hostile to literacy, Christianity embraced it.

Living in small communities and on farms, the Irish did not form a nation in our modern sense. Minor kings ruled fragmented territories, and constant wars among neighboring kings precluded national unity. Ireland had been free of invasion since prehistoric times, but in the ninth century the era of Viking expansion began. The Vikings came from Scandanavia; they were pirates and traders. They slaughtered the people of Ireland and plundered its monasteries. Norsemen set up a fortress at Dublin in 840, and the Danes established a settlement at Waterford in 853 called Vadrefjord. One result of these invasions was the emergence for defensive purposes of a High King, the most notable of which was Brian Boru, who in 1002 was acknowledged "Emperor of the Irish" by all but the Irish Kingdom of Leinster.

More than one hundred years later Dermot MacMurrough, King of Leinster, asked King Henry II of England for military aid in a feud with his neighboring Irish kings, the antagonism caused initially by Dermot's abduction of another king's wife. Dermot's invitation initiated the Norman invasion of Ireland, and for eight centuries his name has been cursed for the troubles he started. Henry, however, had already received from Pope Adrian IV—the only Englishman to be elected pope—an edict authorizing Henry to undertake the conquest of Ireland to "restrain the downward course of vice, correct evil customs, and plant virtue" among the "rude, ignorant, vicious" people of Ireland. Thus it is probable that Henry would have entered Ireland with or without Dermot's invitation.

For more than four hundred years Ireland was more or less ruled by England. Various kings tried to ensure the subjugation of the Irish, but other matters—such as the Hundred Years' War and the War of the Roses—sometimes prevented English royalty from giving proper attention to the control of their neighbors. The animosity between the English and the Irish received a new dimension when Britain became a Protestant country. The English were viewed as heretics by the Roman Catholic Irish, giving rebellion against them a new legitimacy. Four rebellions in the sixteenth century culminated in the victory of the English at Kinsale in 1601. In the aftermath, most of the Irish nobility escaped to Europe in what became known as The Flight of the Earls. The vast tracts of land they left behind in Ulster were divided into "plantations" and awarded to immigrants from England and Scotland. The great influx at that time accounts for the preponderance of Protestants in the North today.

On January 30, 1649, Oliver Cromwell supervised the beheading of King Charles I of England. The monarchy and the House of Lords were abolished, and England was declared to be a commonwealth. In retaliation for the Catholic Rebellion of 1641 in which thousands of Protestants were killed throughout Ireland, Cromwell sought to secure the land for the new republic of England. In the fall of 1649 he massacred several thousand men and women in Drogheda and Wexford. He was systematically and passionately anti-Catholic, stating, "I meddle not with any man's conscience, but if by liberty of conscience you mean a liberty to exercise the Mass, I judge it best to use plain dealing, and to let you know, where the Parliament of England have power, that will not be allowed."

By 1653 Cromwell had subjugated most of Ireland and confiscated the land to provide further "plantations" for his own soldiers. In 1641 Catholics had held three fifths of the land in Ireland; by 1655 they held only one fifth. Ireland was now ruled by Protestants mostly from England and Scotland with the Gaelic-speaking Roman Catholic Irish forming a potentially explosive peasantry, but an important labor force. The next two hundred years were ones of suppression by the British Protestants and rebellion by

BOY SHOVELING DIRT/*Ballyhack*

14

the Irish Catholics. The Penal Laws (1695-1829) put numerous restrictions on Catholics, forbade the Mass, and had the effect of passing most of the land still owned by Catholics into Protestant hands.

In 1845 the Irish peasants' existence was completely tied to the potato, which Sir Walter Raleigh had brought from North Carolina to Ireland in 1585. The peasants had enough to eat when the crop was good, but they starved when it failed. There had been potato crop failures in 1817 and 1822, but no one was prepared for the disastrous series of events starting with a severe blight—caused by a fungus—that occurred first in 1845, followed by an even worse blight in 1846, after which came the harshest winter in memory, another blight in 1848, and another disastrous winter. In 1845 Ireland contained nearly nine million people. In 1851 the population was only 6.5 million, and in 1881 it was just five million. More than one million people died. The rest emigrated. Today there are only 4.3 million people in Ireland—half the population of 1845. Between 1846 and 1891 three million Irish emigrated to America. The famine was a turning point in Irish history. Undoubtedly people become a bit more serious, a bit more resolved when their number is halved.

Increased demand for home rule for Ireland caused more rebellion, more fighting, more bloodshed. In 1913 home rule was resisted by the Ulster Volunteers, who wanted to maintain ties with England. The Anglo-Irish Treaty giving home rule to the twenty-six southern counties was signed on December 6, 1921, establishing the Irish Free State—amidst a civil war that ended in 1923. A new constitution in 1937 renamed the country Ireland (Eire), and in 1949 Ireland left the Commonwealth, a symbolically important act.

Ireland is divided into thirty-two counties in four historic provinces: Munster (six counties) in the south, Leinster (twelve counties) in the east, Connacht (five counties) in the west, and Ulster (nine counties) in the north. Six of the nine counties of Ulster currently constitute Northern Ireland and are a part of the United Kingdom, while counties Donegal, Monaghan, and Cavan are part of the Republic in the south.

Ireland is a land of two governments. In 1969 violence erupted in Derry, Northern Ireland, after years of simmering discontent by northern Catholics who were never happy to have remained under British rule and with what they considered minority status in their own country. Terrorist activities of the Irish Republican Army (which has attempted to force the creation of a United Ireland), the Ulster Defense Association (a Protestant group loyal to Britain), and the introduction of British troops into Northern Ireland have escalated the conflict.

Exploring Eire

My first-hand acquaintance with Ireland began one February when I went to find a cottage in which my family could live—for as long as we needed. I intended to explore the country from one end to the other, learning about the people and capturing the melancholy beauty of the

CHICKENS ON HAYSTACK/*Holy Cross*

island. February is the coldest month of the year in Ireland, and when I arrived a chilled dampness permeated the foggy air. But Ireland has one of the most varied and unpredictable climates in the world; the next day was crisply beautiful.

And green. Ireland's countryside is the deepest and most vivid green I have ever seen. This presented certain problems as I tried to reproduce the vividness on canvas, for when I approached duplicating what I saw, it looked too much like artificial grass. And yet a normally green field in a painting looks washed out in comparison with what is seen in real life. I was probably most successful in portraying this greenness in the painting "Cows in Field."[2]

At the suggestion of a motherly Irish lady who had sat by me on the plane, I went first to County Galway in the west. I spent the night in the city of Galway, and the next day explored the western half of the county, a rugged and mountainous section called Connemara. Galway is a seacoast town and the place where the term "to lynch" originated when the mayor, James Lynch Fitzstephen, condemned and hung his own son for killing a Spanish guest in a fit of jealousy. Connemara is a different world. It's not lush and green, but rocky, desolate, barren, grand, and beautiful. This "stony district" has "too few trees to hang a man, too little water to drown one, too little earth to bury one," according to Cromwell's men. Everywhere one looks, it seems, rock walls built without mortar climb over hills and divide fields. These wonderful walls are sometimes the only evidence that man has been there. They are so pervasive that looking across a field from a distance, one will see only rocks—not the field.

Thirty miles out to sea from Galway, the three Aran Islands bear a striking resemblance to Connemara. These islands are covered with miles of rock walls and meager plots of land which have been painstakingly cultivated for generations. The islanders haul seaweed and sand by hand to enrich the soil and even create soil where there is none. They make their living by farming the sparse acres and by fishing in currachs, a boat of ancient design made of laths and tarred canvas. I watched a man building a currach and was able to sketch a study of him.[3]

In addition to their strange, eerie beauty, both Connemara and the Aran Islands are distinguished by their closeness to the past. Every school child throughout the Republic of Ireland is required to learn Irish (Gaelic). But in Connemara and on the Aran Islands, it is spoken, and the songs and stories of these people enshrine much of Ireland's folklore and culture. Here are the ancient Celtic traditions of Ireland preserved in their purest form. Connemara and the Aran Islands are beautiful not only for their ruggedly spectacular scenery, but because of the way they have preserved the magic and culture of the Irish Celtic past.

Although Connemara is one of the most beloved sections of Ireland, I

2. COWS IN FIELD/*County Derry,* page 104.
3. MAKING A CURRACH/*The Aran Islands,* page 124.

decided not to take a cottage there because it is not typical of the Irish countryside. I had an idealistic vision of what I was looking for: A little white cottage with a thatched roof and smoke wisping out of the chimney, set in acres of pasture land overlooking the ocean with waves crashing against the rocks. I visualized driving my family up a lane bordered by thistle hedges. Coming to the top of a slight hill, we would see the white cottage framed on the bottom by the lushest green on earth and on the top by a blue Irish sky.

I never decided whether my romanticism was that of an artist or a tourist, but it was very important to me that our cottage should have a thatched roof. There are many new traditional type cottages in Ireland, but a new thatched roof is a rarity since the art of thatching seems to be gradually disappearing. The farmer in Lady's Island who patiently posed for me on his ladder[4] explained that for years he had tried to get his farmhouse re-thatched. Finally he decided to learn how to do it himself.

County Kerry in the extreme southwest—where I visited next—is the only other part of Ireland that can match Connemara for its wild beauty and Gaelic-speaking people. Its coastline is formed by three large peninsulas which alternate sandy bays with rocky cliffs and caves. Here is some of the finest scenery in the British Isles, but even with its importance as a resort area, the modern world seems to threaten the past with only slightly more vigor than in Connemara or on the Aran Islands. Considered the most beautiful drive in Ireland, the Ring of Kerry Road around the Iveragh Peninsula displays luxuriant vegetation and ancient trees contrasted against the muted tones of the mountain ranges that sometimes dip into the sea.[5] The Dingle Peninsula contains more ruins of old stone fortresses and monastic settlements than anywhere else in Ireland. The Gallarus Oratory, an early Christian church, is remarkably well-preserved. Although it was built of unmortared stone more than one thousand years ago, it is still water tight. Dingle has a primitive beauty. I later painted a picture of some children on a beach in Dingle in which I took particular care to try to catch the mist that was rising out of the mountains.[6]

Driving north, I considered an apartment in a huge old manor house. It was owned by a man whose portrait I sketched, calling him "Gentleman Farmer."[7] He said that he had inherited this great house and several hundred acres of land. He was running a dairy farm; his wife was renting out part of the house to tourists. The man was tall and didn't speak with a brogue. I encountered this lack of accent several times, and the answer to my query was always the same—"we're educated Irish," always said matter-of-factly. The house was stately with the entrance hall dominated by a grand stairway flanked with a polished railing and large, ornately-framed portraits. It is not unusual for a magnificent house filled with elegant furni-

4. ROOF THATCHING/*Lady's Island*, page 21.
5. SEA GULLS/*Ring of Kerry*, pages 18-19.
6. WALKING ON THE BEACH/*Dingle*, pages 122-123.
7. GENTLEMAN FARMER/*Puckane*, page 41.

SEA GULLS/*Ring of Kerry*

ture to be owned by someone of more modest means than the house would suggest. Ireland has thousands of such houses, and they are often viewed as white elephants. At one time the government put a tax on any building that had a complete roof. The predictable happened: any house—including many great houses—that was not being used had part of its roof torn off to save taxes.

One such tragic example was the Johnstown House in Tipperary; its shell had been demolished the year before I arrived. Dating from the seventeenth century, it had been the manor house for thousands of acres. So many workers were required then to till the land that a cow was slaughtered each day to feed them lunch. Now only the imposing entry gate is left standing. In the 1930s the house was sold in good condition to a local speculator who wanted to dismantle it and sell the excellent timbers in the roof. However, the house was so sturdy and difficult to destroy that after his expenses, he lost money and Ireland lost a beautiful house.[8] Before 1973 it was possible to buy a great house with a little land quite reasonably. But since Ireland joined the Common Market and thereby found expanded markets for its agricultural products, the value of land has escalated considerably.

I next visited County Wexford in the southeastern corner of the country. Wexford's history goes back to pre-Christian times, but it is the fighting of the pikemen from Wexford in the Rebellion of 1798 that is the most memorable part of its history. Although a guidebook said that "since the southern and western coasts are even more beautiful and rich in character than those in the east, there is little to be lost" by not visiting Wexford, it was one of my favorite parts of the country, probably because memories are made not of scenery and architecture, but of people. Later one of our most pleasant experiences as a family was staying for a week in a beautiful Georgian home with fan windows above the doors overlooking the River Barrow near Dunganstown in Wexford, less than a mile from the cottage which was the birthplace of the great-grandfather of John, Robert, and Ted Kennedy. The house was owned by a young couple who had children[9] the ages of ours. Michael Ryan was an announcer on Irish television in Dublin, eighty-five miles away, and Anne[10] ran their home as a guest house for part of the year. They were spunky and hard working.

We lived in two large, airy rooms, ate exquisite meals, and were treated as part of the family. One evening, Michael made a point of introducing me to an old fisherman in a pub in Arthurstown. This man looked like what I imagine a leprechaun to be, and I feel his portrait is one of the best I painted.[11]

Michael and Anne Ryan's house is typical of many guest houses in Ireland and Britain, although there is a great variety in the quality of them. Guest houses are private homes or farm houses that have rooms available

8. JOHNSTOWN HOUSE RUINS/*County Tipperary,* page 58.
9. CHILDREN WITH GOAT/*River Barrow,* pages 134-135.
10. SITTING BY A WINDOW/*Killowen House,* page 96.
11. PUB SCENE/*Arthurstown,* pages 84-85.

ROOF THATCHING/*Lady's Island*

Gordon Wetmore ©1979

CARRYING STRAW TO ROOF/*Lady's Island*

for rent. Guidebooks list hundreds of such homes, offering an inexpensive and friendly vacation. What is characteristic of a stay in a guest house is that you are made to feel part of the family and receive very personal service. I remember one cold night in an unheated guest house. Mrs. Brennan, the owner, gave us all hot water bottles. The next morning our children watched her daughter feed the pigs while I sketched the house.[12] In another instance, I stayed two or three days with an American couple—the wife's parents had both been born in Ireland and the husband had originally come from Ireland—who had raised their children in Boston and had returned to Ireland every year for a vacation. Eventually they bought a large Gothic style house with some land, repaired it, and then moved there because they liked the freedom from pressures. She ran their home as a guest house, and he ran the farm, a fairly common combination.

Returning from Wexford, I passed through Kilkenny, a beautiful city of narrow, winding streets and old buildings including one of the prettiest castles in all Ireland.[13] Originally built in the thirteenth century, Kilkenny Castle has been almost entirely restored.

Driving towards Shannon Airport, I entered County Tipperary, which I came to love as one of the most beautiful parts of Ireland. It is the heart of the island, bordered by the River Shannon. It was at Cashel in Tipperary that St. Patrick is said to have used the shamrock to explain the doctrine of the Trinity, thus giving Ireland one of its most famous symbols. I had decided that I should look for a cottage nearer to Shannon Airport since that is where planes from America land and I knew we would be making a few trips to the airport. I wanted to be away from civilization, but not too far from a store. And I still had my vision of a thatched white cottage. Just before returning to America, I found what I was looking for. It had a thatched roof, was in the middle of the country, not too far from the town of Nenagh, overlooked Lough Derg, one of Ireland's principal trout lakes, and was beautifully maintained. There was a sun room on the back with glass on three sides from which I felt I could see all of Ireland. There is a feeling of bigness in Ireland—big land, big sky—and the view overlooking Lough Derg from the back of this house typified it. The house was on a hill and a lack of trees allowed a view of miles of rolling gentle land. At one time Ireland had many more trees than it does now, but the English cut them for their own use. Constant grazing prevents reforestation. I took some pictures, returned to America, and called the owners to reserve the cottage.[14]

Living in Ireland

We arrived soon afterwards—my wife, Connie, five-year-old Amy, our baby Alexandra, an eleven-year-old friend named Charlie, and myself—with enough baggage to last us for a number of months. Bringing my family

12. BRENNAN FARM/*Glen of Aherlow*, page 137.
13. KILKENNY CASTLE/*Kilkenny*, page 24.
14. JOHNSOWN COTTAGE/*Lough Derg*, page 28.

KILKENNY CASTLE/*Kilkenny*

BIRR CASTLE/*Birr*

to the cottage was just as I had envisioned it. Amy joyfully described the cottage as a "Three-Little-Pig house." Connie liked the seeming isolation—from the back, the only structures in sight were a distant farmhouse and the ruins of an ancient Norman keep, a high square tower that once served as a fortified castle.

We quickly became acquainted with the surrounding area and met our neighbors, the Gleesons, a hardworking family with three girls and six boys. The men worked in the field, the women in the house. At four each afternoon they gathered in their kitchen for tea. I was fascinated by their kitchen—the center of their house—but it wasn't until nearly the end of our visit that I finally painted a picture of it, complete with shirts hanging over the stove to dry.[15]

The Gleeson boys taught Charlie how to play hurling, a tremendously fast game played with four-foot curved sticks, a bit like hockey. Hurling, Gaelic football (similar to soccer except that the players can use their hands), and handball are regulated by the Gaelic Athletic Association which preserves and popularizes native Irish pastimes. Horse racing is another important sport in Ireland. Horseback riding lessons became part of our weekly routine, and we enjoyed attending "point to point" races, which are conducted on a large open field rather than on an enclosed track.[16]

The owner of our cottage, Paddy Cadell,[17] was the proprietor of the Hibernian Inn, a pub in Nenagh. The word *Hibernian* refers to anything Irish and is a name used by many establishments all over Ireland. Pubs have a unique place in Irish life. Every village has at least one, and at four o'clock men from fields and villages can be seen drifting towards the pub. Families also gather in pubs, and Paddy's fourteen-year-old son John frequently tended bar. The reputation that the Irish have for enjoying a drink makes it interesting that there is an active temperance organization in which many school children as well as adults are enthusiastic members.

Part of the Irish mystique is usually held to be the gregariousness and loquaciousness that is found in the pubs—fully developed, of course, by much strong drink. It's not just the number of words that sets the Irish apart, but their wit, their skill in turning a phrase, their love of a good story, their poetic bent that sees as much beauty in the abstractness of language as in the tangibleness of a mountain. It is the Irish who value poets and artists enough to allow them to live tax free within their borders. This love of words can be traced back to the ancient Celts.

The American writer J. P. Donleavy, who now lives in Ireland, says that in pubs "people consciously get on a stage and take on starring roles." He says that Ireland is famous for producing novelists and poets, "but the writers are failed talkers and people who can't stand on their own in the pubs." Whether Irish writers are "failed talkers" or not, the country has produced many notable novelists, poets, dramatists, and orators including Jonathan Swift, Oliver Goldsmith, Oscar Wilde, George Bernard Shaw,

15. AFTERNOON TEA/*Gleeson Farm*, page 86.
16. POINT TO POINT/*Thurles*, page 143.
17. PADDY CADDELL/*Nenagh*, page 92.

YOUNG GIRL/*Tralee*

27

William Butler Yeats, Sean O'Casey, James Joyce, Samuel Beckett, and Brendan Behan.

Many of these literary giants came from Dublin and account for its being as much a state of mind as a city, for Dubliners are ever mindful of their reputation as wits and writers as well as talkers and drinkers. I didn't spend much time in Dublin, for I wanted to experience rural Ireland. While Dublin seems very Irish, it is as characteristic of Ireland as New York City is of America or London is of England. The height of Dublin's glory was in the eighteenth century, and its finest homes and most noble buildings date from that period when Dublin was considered one of the glittering cities in Europe. Nobility, intellectuals, and people of fashion all flocked to Dublin to promenade in the elegant squares and gather behind the tall candle-lit windows and fan-lighted doors. The world premier of Handel's *Messiah* was held in 1724 in Dublin's Musick Hall with the composer himself conducting. Recent growth around the city has been large, but the center of Dublin today still has a small city intimacy not usually associated with European capitals.[18]

Northern Ireland is the focal point of the tensions that have plagued the Irish since the days of Henry II. It is a separate political entity from the Republic in the south, but the two areas are both very Irish. They have a common history. They are one people. True, there are differences: The six counties of Northern Ireland are more industrialized and more densely populated than the south, they have a more British character to them, and they are two thirds Protestant while the south is ninety percent Catholic. But it is one Ireland, even though the differences are emphasized by a well-guarded frontier.

Unfortunately, what one remembers about the urban areas of Northern Ireland is the tension, although the rural areas are as peaceful as the south. The center of Belfast, however, is protected by high fences and guards stationed at every building's entrance. One day I got lost there and parked my car to walk to a guard post to ask directions. I didn't think it unusual that mine was the only car parked on the street. However, when the guards saw it, they dashed over and started searching the car for a bomb. It's frightening to realize that they weren't playing games. After getting my directions, I drove past a fruit stand that was particularly colorful. I stopped and walked across the street with a telephoto lens on my camera to wait for the right moment to take some pictures. In about fifteen minutes two characters who had been drinking walked by, thought I looked suspicious, and angrily demanded identification. I explained that I was an artist, but since I wasn't carrying any papers that would verify my occupation, I had no luck convincing them that my presence was harmless. They were finally satisfied when I showed them my Tennessee driver's license. I was shaken. When I got back in the car I looked up to see an armored car turning the corner towards me with a soldier standing in the back cradling a gun in his arms. My instinct said to pick up my telephoto and shoot him, but I

JOHNSTOWN COTTAGE/*Lough Derg*

18. DUBLIN STREET SCENE/*Dublin*, pages 34-35.

didn't. I'm afraid his instinct, living with constant tension, would have told him to shoot me also.

Belfast is the capital of Northern Ireland[19] and an important shipbuilding center. It was here that the *Titanic* was built in 1911, which the Irish from the south claimed was sunk by a thunderbolt from God because the mirror image of its alleged number, 390,904, looked suspiciously like the slogan "No Pope." Much of Belfast retains signs in its architecture of its essentially industrial nature, architecture which has been referred to as "Victorian grisly." Near Belfast is Lough Neagh, the largest lake in Ireland or Britain.

Derry, Northern Ireland's second largest city, is very attractive with many hilly streets. Originally it was named just "Derry"—the name still used by most Irish—but in the seventeenth century it was given to the city of London to manage and the name was lengthened to Londonderry. On the day I arrived, people were preparing the downtown area for St. Patrick's Day.[20] Many of the disturbances in Northern Ireland have been centered in Derry, since the military presence is very obvious there. When I crossed the border just outside of Derry into Donegal, I photographed a guard. As a result the soldiers spent half an hour searching my car thoroughly.

Donegal is the most northern county in Ireland. Although it is a part of Ulster, it is not one of the six counties of Northern Ireland. When I visited Northern Ireland I also wanted to drive around this remote and mysterious area. All along the west coast of Donegal imposing cliffs plunge straight into the sea. I was told that five tons of gold lie off this coast near Burtonport in a sunken ship from the Spanish Armada. In the center of Lough Derg (a different lake, but with the same name as the one behind our Irish home) is one of Ireland's most celebrated holy places. A very early legend says that through forty days of prayer and fasting St. Patrick expelled evil spirits who had infested the cave on the island. In the Middle Ages, the story spread and grew, and the island became the object of many pilgrimages, as it is today. The devout may make a three-day pilgrimage during which time they must go barefoot and take only one meal per day of bread and black tea.

The Hibernian Balm

POPE JOHN PAUL II
LIMERICK
1979

For more than four months we lived in Ireland, traveling over narrow roads from Kerry to Donegal and from Mayo to Wexford. We took a small open boat from near the Cliffs of Moher to the Aran Islands to visit those lonely rocky places where Gaelic is still spoken. We stopped in modern, urban cities, but even in Dublin there is an unhurriedness that is characteristically Irish. If a Dubliner meets a friend on the street, he is sure to stop to talk and maybe even take the time for a cup of coffee or a drink —or several. It is this charm, this balanced way of living, that I remember about Ireland. I like to think that like those who have tried to conquer Ireland, I too have been conquered by it.

19. ROOFTOPS/*Belfast,* pages 108-109.
20. HANGING BANNERS/*Derry,* page 102.

POPE JOHN PAUL II/*Limerick*

For years irritableness and impatience had been a thorn in my flesh. Prayers and efforts at reform failed to remove it. But during the time I lived in Ireland I changed. I've searched my memory to try to pinpoint when the balm took effect, only to realize that my agitation left me a little each day. It hasn't returned because I can readily recall experiencing the Irish mystique and my frustrations are put into perspective. The Irish have retained a quality in the pace of their living which produces a relaxed, pressure-free environment, a relief from the perils of much of civilization: suspicion, pressure, materialism.

It has been said that Ireland is a land of too many ideals and too much religion. And yet why is it that so many who have visited there find a longing in themselves to return to the beauty of Ireland—not just the beauty of the land, for that can be equalled in many places throughout the world, but the beauty of the people? Perhaps the rest of the world is a land of too few ideals and too little religion.

MAN CUTTING PEAT/County Galway

MORNING CHORES/*Glen of Aherlow*

THE HEARTLAND
FROM DUBLIN TO TIPPERARY

In Dublin's fair city, where girls are so pretty
I first set my eyes on sweet Molly Malone.
She wheeled her wheelbarrow through streets wide and narrow,
Crying, "Cockles and mussels, alive, alive, oh!
Alive, Alive, Oh!
Alive, Alive, Oh!"
Crying, "Cockles and mussels, alive, alive oh!"

ANONYMOUS
19th century

DUBLIN STREET SCENE/*Dublin*

34

Gordon Wetmore
© 1980

Often in the evening when the stars were still pale in the sky, the boys would see the girls skipping at the other end of the street, as many as ten or fifteen of them jumping gracefully over a regularly turning rope. The boys would slink up nearer and nearer to the skipping girls, the girls would occasionally glance disdainfully at the boys, but in their hearts they wished them to come closer. With a defiant shout, weakened with the tones of a shy shame in it, a boy, bolder than the rest, would jump in merrily; the rest would follow him, and joyous faces of boys and girls would shine out of thin dusty clouds raised out of the road by the beating of the skippers' feet dancing in the way of peace. Tired of skipping, someone would suggest a ring; and boys and girls, their shyness gone, would join hands in a great ring . . . with arms held high while a player would dart in and out of the ring under the upraised arms as the circle of boys and girls sang

Chase him all round Dublin, chase him all round
Dublin, chase him all round Dublin,
As you have done before.

SEAN O'CASEY

BOYS DELIVERING MILK ON CART/*Castleconnell*

SCHOOLBOY/Puckane

37

Come with me, under my coat
And we will drink our fill
Of the milk of the white goat,
Or wine if it be thy will.

And we will talk, until
Talk is a trouble, too,
Out on the side of the hill;
And nothing is left to do.

But an eye to look into an eye;
And a hand in a hand to slip,
And a sigh to answer a sigh;
And a lip to find out a lip!

What if the night is black!
Or the air on the mountain chill!
Where the goat lies down in her track,
And all but the fern is still!

Stay with me, under my coat!
And we will drink our fill
Of the milk of the white goat,
Out on the side of the hill!

OLD CONNACHT LYRIC
Translated by James Stephens

MAN STANDING IN CART/*Nenagh*

For the great earls of Ireland
Are the men that God made mad.
For all their wars are merry
And all their songs are sad.

G. K. CHESTERTON

GENTLEMAN FARMER/*Puckane*

A PRIEST INSISTING ON HIS RIGHTS

One of the strangest stories that I ever heard came from the lips of a bishop, the late Dr. Lyons of Kilmore, who referred me to the Bishop of Galway. He had heard it at the same time when the story was told at Maynooth in 1935 by the priest who brought the Irish setter dog mentioned [in the story] into the American mission field, the scene of the story. The tale ran:

An Irish priest received his first appointment as pastor in a small parish some distance from civilization. His predecessor was an old Irish priest, Father D— —. He had not died there, but had been taken to a hospital. Through some mistake on the part of the diocesan office, his successor, Father O'F— —, was appointed as pastor, not as administrator. As apparently the man was still alive, they took it that it would be only a matter of a short time until he died. The old man lived for some time after the other was appointed to his parish. He seems to have been insistent on his rights as Parish Priest, as he expressed a definite desire that on his death his remains should be brought back to his parish church, left there for one night, and then brought back to some church in the city where his funeral could be more conveniently attended by the clergy. The old man died, and his wishes were not carried out. Through some oversight, or because it was too much trouble, his remains were not brought to the church for the customary night before the altar. Hence, not merely had he been deprived of his right and title as P.P. by the precipitate appointment of a successor, but he had been denied the traditional favour of resting before the altar where he had been P.P.

His successor had made several visits to Ireland since his appointment. On returning after his last visit he brought back with him a magnificent red setter dog. Shortly after his predecessor died, the dog began to make himself a nuisance by howling in a most disturbing manner at night. Every night he kept up this mournful howling, to the great surprise of the P.P., who, however, was a man of very sound nerves. Then, on the Saturday after his annual retreat, he came back to his parish from the city, heard confessions, locked the front door of the church, put out the main switch, and previous to leaving through the sacristy, knelt for a few moments in the dark before the high altar. Suddenly the lights went on, the front door opened, and he heard the click as the leaves of the door swung back into their catches. He looked around and saw a coffin coming up the middle passage supported on nothing, but about two or three feet from the ground. He fled through the sacristy to his house, which stood beside the church. As he rushed through the front room of the house he glanced out through the window at the church; the lights were out. In the morning there was no sign of the doors having been opened.

Some days passed, and nothing happened, but the setter kept up the howling. Then one morning, after early Mass, he was kneeling in the church, making his thanksgiving. He had to say Mass early, as the few who

CELTIC CROSS/*Clonmacnois*

attended it had to get early into the city. He was alone in the church; it was a fine, warm morning in July. Suddenly he heard the doors of the church swing open and the lights went on: he looked back, and there again he saw the coffin coming up the central passage. This time he felt no panic. The coffin stood supported on air in front of the altar. He got up from his knees, went to the sacristy, put on soutane, surplice and stole, took his ritual and the holy water, came out and stood before the altar. He read the prayers which are said for the Absolution when a body is removed from the church for burial. Then he walked round the coffin sprinkling it with holy water. As he did so, he noticed that the head of the coffin was towards the altar, according to the canonical custom, in the case of a priest, and that the name on the breastplate was that of his predecessor. He finished the prayers calmly and walked back to the sacristy. The coffin withdrew, and he heard the doors closing. That night the setter did not howl or any night after.

SHANE LESLIE
Ghost Book

LITTLE GIRL OFFERING FLOWERS
TO WOMAN ON BIKE/County Tipperary

LITTLE BOY AND OLD MAN READING PAPER/*Limerick*

BOY IN DOORWAY/*Puckane*

45

Gordon Wetmore
© 1979

MAN DRIVING CATTLE/*County Tipperary*

RUSTY MILK CAN/*County Tipperary*

Grey brick upon brick,
Declammatory bronze
On somber pedestals—
O'Connell, Grattan, Moore—
And the brewery tugs and the swans
On the balustrated stream
And the bare bones of a fanlight—
Over a hungry door
And the air soft on the cheek
And porter running from the taps
With a head of yellow cream
And Nelson on his pillar
Watching his world collapse.

LOUIS MACNEICE
"Dublin"

O'CONNELL STREET BRIDGE/*Dublin*

ST. PATRICK'S DAY
PARADE

NENAGH
1979

Where dips the rocky highland
Of Sleuth Wood in the lake,
There lies a leafy island
Where flapping herons wake
The drowsy water-rats;
There we've hid our faery vats,
Full of berries
And of the reddest stolen cherries.
Come away, O human child!
To the waters and the wild
With a faery, hand in hand,
For the world's more full of weeping than you can understand.

W. B. YEATS
"The Stolen Child"

COTTAGE WITH RED DOOR/*Puckane*

51

I will arise and go now, and go to Innisfree,
And a small cabin build there, of clay and wattles made;
Nine bean rows will I have there,
 a hive for the honey bee,
And live alone in the bee-loud glade.
And I shall have some peace there, for
 peace comes dropping slow,
Dropping from the veils of the morning
 to where the cricket sings;
There midnight's all a glimmer and
 noon a purple glow,
And evening full of the limmet's wings.
I will arise and go now, for always night
 and day
I hear lake water lapping with low
 sounds by the shore;
While I stand on the roadway, or on
 the pavements grey,
I hear it in the deep heart's core.

W. B. YEATS
"The Lake Isle of Innisfree"

COW SHED/*County Tipperary*

53

May the wisdom of God instruct you.
May the eye of God watch over you.
May the ear of God hear you.
May the hand of God defend you.
May the way of God guide you.

ST. PATRICK

NENAGH STREET SCENE/*Nenagh*

IRISH NUN/*Ballyneety*

55

Inevitably, there is a legend about
the origin of the Shannon—going back
once again to the Tuatha De Danann and
the daughter of their great sea king, Lir.
At that time Connia's well, which has long since
vanished, teemed with salmon, and the
fish fed on nuts from the hazel trees
overhanging the water. The nuts had the
property of wisdom, and the salmon which ate them
were distinguished by brilliant crimson spots;
whoever ate these salmon became wise in turn.
Women were forbidden within the precincts
of the well, but the king's daughter, Sinnan, who was
already beautiful and accomplished, was
determined to be as wise as the men of her
father's court. She made her way stealthily towards
the well, but as soon as she approached
the edge, the water surged up and overwhelmed her;
her drowned body was born along by the
current as the water poured out of the well for
ever and rushed through the countryside to form
what is now the River Shannon.

THORNTON COX
Travellers' Guide to Ireland

BRINGING IN THE CATCH/*Shannon River*

JOHNSTOWN HOUSE RUINS/*County Tipperary*

A stone's throw from an old house where I spent several summers
in County Wicklow, there was a garden that had been left to itself
for fifteen or twenty years.... Everyone is used in Ireland to the tragedy
that is bound up with the lives of farmers and fishing people;
but in this garden one seemed to feel the tragedy of the landlord class also,
and of the innumerable old families that are quickly dwindling away.
These owners of the land are not much pitied at the present day,
or much deserving of pity; and yet one cannot quite forget that
they are the descendants of what was at one time, in the
eighteenth century, a high-spirited and highly cultivated aristocracy.
The broken green-houses and mouse-eaten libraries that were
designed and collected by men who voted with Gratten are perhaps
as mournful in the end as the four mud walls that are so often left
in Wicklow as the only remnants of a farmhouse.

J. M. SYNGE
"A Landlord's Garden in County Wicklow"

BOY LYING IN FIELD/*Lough Derg*

THE WEST
STRANGE AND BEAUTIFUL

WOOL BASKET/*Sligo*

My house . . . stands on a lake, but it stands also on the sea.
Water-lilies meet the golden seaweed.
It is as if, in the fairy land of Connemara at the extreme end of Europe,
the incongruous flowed together at last; and the sweet and bitter blended.

OLIVER ST. JOHN GOGARTY
As I Was Going Down Sackville Street

BOY WITH DONKEY/*Costelloe*

...No one who knew the meaning of nationality found it difficult to understand
that the Irish had, in past centuries, resisted conquest and absorption
by another race; what caused astonishment, whether hostile or sympathetic, was
the passion and tenacity with which the resistance had been maintained.

The explanation of that resistance, continued through centuries, lies in
instincts so simple that political sophists overlook them at times—
the instincts of race, of religion, and of a people's right to its land.
Three facts gave the Irish struggle its enduring force: the facts that an
ancient Gaelic people was resisting a race whose civilisation was antipathetic
to its own, that a Catholic nation was defending its faith against
the forces of Protestantism, and that under George the Fifth as under Elizabeth,
English rule meant dispossession and humiliation for the Irish on their own soil.

DOROTHY MACARDLE
The Irish Republic

CHURCH/Donegal

Outside Cahersiveen on the northern arch of the Ring road, the peak of Knocknadober looms up between the road and the sea. In pagan days Lughnasa, the harvest festival, was celebrated on its summit. In Christian times the mountain's sacred well was dedicated to Fursa, an Irish saint of visions, and became a place of pilgrimage. Just before Glenbeigh the Ring passes through Mountain Stage, where Synge stayed in Philly Harris' cottage, and then runs on to Killorglin.

Once a year, not long before the harvest, Puck Fair happens in Killorglin. Men of the town set out for MacGillycuddy's Reeks, the magnificent range to the south, one of whose peaks—Carrantuohill, "the Left-handed Reaping Hook"—is the highest in Ireland. They snare the largest, handsomest he-goat they can find and bear him back, rearing, charging, kicking, but unharmed, to Killorglin.

By late afternoon of "Gathering Day" (usually August 10), the narrow, old-world streets are achingly full, mottled crowds streaming back and forth, catching sparks of rising anticipation. Expatriate children from England and America stride by, their foreign finery a show of success. Itinerant fiddlers and blind balladeers from all over Ireland pass the hat at every corner. Men with swift, trembling hands encourage you to choose a card, any card, from an ancient deck. The tinkers, the people of the roads, are here, for above all this is their festival: the women, each wrapped in a plaid shawl which hides a bundle or a baby, sell their trinkets and beg for the price of a loaf or a bottle of stout; the men display young horses and old furniture, and haggle with Kerry farmers; the children, ragged and wary, supplement their parents' income by keeping an eye out for accessible pockets and handbags. The Pecker Dunn, the bard of the Travelling People (as the tinkers call themselves), will almost certainly be here. A great, swarthy man, a ferocious gypsy, he will play his fiddle over his head and behind his back, and sing in a voice to make you shiver. His delicate, beautiful wife will pass a tankard that will quickly fill with silver. She is no gypsy, they will whisper in the audience, but a girl from good stock with a university degree and whatever you please. She left all to follow the gypsy rover.

SUSAN AND THOMAS CAHILL
A Literary Guide to Ireland

TINKER BOY/*County Kerry*

67

TINKERS/County Kerry

The worst vice is slight compared with the guiltiness of
a man or woman who defies the central order of the world. . . .
The only truth a wave knows is that it is going to break.
The only truth a bud knows is that it is going to expand and flower.
The only truth we know is that we are a flood
of magnificent life, the fruit of some frenzy of the earth.

J. M. SYNGE
When the Moon Has Set

SHEEPDOG/*Waterville*

69

Gordon Wetmore

The earth alone supplies us with food, let us cling closely to it,
and not quit it. The landlord or agent bids us depart—let us stay.
The Courts of Justice order it—still let us stay.
An armed force is sent to compel us—let us resist it.
Let us oppose all our forces to an unjust force, and in order that
the injustice should not reach us, let us exact the
most terrible penalties against those by whom it is committed.

GUSTAVE DE BEAUMONT
"The White Boys"

LONEL COTTAGE/*Maamturk Mountains*

While we honour in song and in story
The names of the patriot men
Whose valour has covered with glory
Full many a mountain and glen,
Forget not the boys of the heather,
Who marshalled their bravest and best
When Ireland lay broken and bleeding.
Hurrah for the men of the West!

The hilltops with glory were glowing,
'Twas the eve of a bright harvest day,
When the ships we've been wearily waiting
Sailed into Killala's broad bay;
And over the hills went the slogan
To waken in every breast
The fire that has never been quenched, boys,
Among the true hearts of the West.

. . . .

Though all the bright dreamings we cherished
Went down in disaster and woe,
The spirit of old is still with us
That never would bend for the foe;
And Connacht is ready whenever
The loud rolling tuck of the drum
Rings out to awaken the echoes
And tell us the morning has come.

TRADITIONAL SONG

MAN WITH SHEEP/*Donegal*

MAN WITH PIPE/*Donegal*

I am of Ireland,
And of the holy land
Of Ireland.
Good Sir, pray I thee,
For of saint charite—
Come and dance with me
In Ireland.

ANONYMOUS
14th century

OLD MAN AND BOY ON CART/*Portumna*

WHITE COTTAGE/*County Clare*

Stony seaboard, far and foreign,
    Stony hills poured over space,
Stony outcrop of the Burren,
    Stones in every fertile place,
Little fields with boulders dotted,
Grey-stone shoulders saffron-spotted,
Stone-walled cabins thatched with reeds,
Where a Stone Age people breeds
    The last of Europe's stone age race.

JOHN BETJEMAN
"Sunday in Ireland"

CONNEMARA PONY/*Inverin*

THE IRISH
A TIMELESS PEOPLE

GIRL BY RED DOOR/*Wexford*

MAN IN PUB/*Arthurstown*

GARDA AND OLD MAN CHATTING ON PARK BENCH/*Kilkenny*

No serpent nor vile venomed thing
Can live upon the Gaelic soil,
No bard nor stranger since has found
A cold repulse from a son of Galedhac.

ANCIENT IRISH

FAMILY IN CART/*Killalee*

CUTTING THATCH/*Bunratty Folk Village*

Gordon Wetmore © 1980

When things go wrong and will not come right
Though you do the best you can,
When life looks black as the hours of night,
A pint of plain is your only man.

When money's tight and is hard to get
And your horse has also ran,
When all you have is a heap of debt
A pint of plain is your only man.

When health is bad and your heart feels strange
And your face is pale and wan,
When doctors say that you need a change
A pint of plain is your only man.

When food is scarce and your larder bare
And no rashers grease your pan,
When hunger grows as your meals grow rare
A pint of plain is your only man.

In time of trouble and lousy strife
You still have got a darling plan,
You still can turn to a brighter life
A pint of plain is your only man.

FLANN O'BRIEN
The Workman's Friend

PUB SCENE/*Arthurstown*

AFTERNOON TEA/*County Tipperary*

The North opens wide the doors of opportunity to every man who comes to its borders with willing hands and eager brain. The South opens a door, too, but it is the door of hospitality, and it bids the stranger enter in, not so much for what he can give, but for what he can take in the way of welcome.

IRWIN S. COBB
Speech to American Irish Historical Society
January 6, 1917

GLEESON BOYS/*County Tipperary*

An ancient bridge, and a more ancient tower,
A farmhouse that is sheltered by its wall,
An acre of stony ground,
Where the symbolic rose can break in flower,
Old ragged elms, old thorns innumerable,
The sound of the rain or sound
Of every wind that blows . . .
A winding stair, a chamber arched with stone,
A grey stone fireplace with an open hearth,
A candle and written page.

W. B. YEATS
"Meditations in Time of Civil War"

GIRL WITH FLOWERS/*Glenbeigh*

Up in the north-east corner of County Cork
is a stretch of limestone country—
open, airy, not quite flat;
it is just perceptibly tilted from north to south,
and the fields undulate in a smooth flowing away.
Dark knolls and screens of trees,
the network of hedges, abrupt stony ridges,
slate glints from roofs give the landscape a featured look
—but the prevailing impression is emptiness.
This is a part of Ireland with no lakes,
but the sky's movement of clouds reflects itself
everywhere as it might on water, rounding the trees
with bloom and giving the grass a sheen.
In the airy silence, any sound travels a long way.
The streams and rivers,
sunk in their valleys,
are not seen until you come down to them.

ELIZABETH BOWEN
Bowen's Court

WOMAN PUSHING CHILD IN CARRIAGE/*Mallow*

GIRL WITH DOG/*County Cork*

PADDY CADDELL/*Nenagh*

Many of the nobles of the English nation and lesser men also had set out thither,
forsaking their native island either for the grace of sacred learning or a more austere life.
And some of them indeed soon dedicated themselves faithfully to the monastic life,
others rejoiced rather to give themselves to learning, going about from one master's cell to another.
All these the Irish willingly received, and saw to it to supply them with food day
by day without cost, and books for their studies and teaching, free of charge.

THE VENERABLE BEDE
Glendalough

MAN PASSING BY MARKET/*Limerick*

GIRL WORKING AT KENNEDY'S STORE/*Puckane*

We are the music-makers
     And we are the dreamers of dreams,
Wandering by lone sea-breakers,
     And sitting by desolate streams;
World-losers and world forsakers
     Of the world forever, it seems.

ARTHUR WILLIAM EDGAR O'SHAUGHNESSY, 1870
"Ode," Stanza I

CHILDREN SWINGING/*Killowen House*   97

From an eminence,
I caught sight not only of a fine view, but
of the most beautiful view I ever saw in the world ...
A miracle of beauty ... the Bay, and the Reek,
which sweeps down to the sea,
and a hundred islands in it, were dressed up
in gold and purple, and crimson, with the whole
cloudy west in a flame. Wonderful, wonderful!

WILLIAM M. THACKERAY
Irish Sketch Book

BRIDGE/*Westport House*

THE NORTH
TENSION AND PEACE

Gordon Wetmore © 1980

The dearest of any on Erin's ground
For its peace and its beauty I gave it my love,
Each leaf of the oaks around Derry is found
To be crowded with angels from Heaven above.

My Derry! My Derry! My little oak grove,
   My dwelling, my home, and my own little cell,
May God the Eternal in Heaven above
   Send death to thy foes and defend thee well.

ST. COLUMCILLE

ARMORED CAR PASSING TAXI/*Belfast*

For the Irish the world is still magical. Mountains and rivers
are named for the banished gods. In many a field stands a faery mound,
which the plowman painstakingly avoids, for he would not risk disturbing it.
For unnumbered centuries barefoot penitents have
climbed jagged hills to inaccessible sanctuaries of pilgrimage.
There are paths no man will cross because of the unbearable hunger that
will seize him, for here the peasants lay down and died in the Great Famine.
Kerry celebrates a yearly fair where a he-goat is exalted on
a platform high above the town in promise of fertility,
and people dance for three nights in the square.
The countryside is dotted with prehistoric stone configurations,
ancient churches, and spectacular, haunted Georgian houses.
Each place has its strange story.

SUSAN AND THOMAS CAHILL
A Literary Guide to Ireland

Gordon Wetmore ©1979

...snow was general all over Ireland.
It was falling on every part of the dark central plain,
on the treeless hills, falling softly upon the Bog of Allen and,
farther westward, softly falling into the dark mutinous Shannon waves.
It was falling, too, upon every part of the lonely churchyard
on the hill where Michael Furey lay buried.
It lay thickly drifted on the crooked crosses and headstones,
on the spears of the little gate, on the barren thorns....

James Joyce
The Dead

BALLYCONNELL SNOW/*County Leitrim*

107

Ireland, with all thy faults, thy follies, too,
I love thee still, still with a candid eye must view
Thy wit too quick, still blundering into sense,
Thy reckless humor, and improvidence,
And even what sober judges follies call . . .
I, looking at the Heart, forget them all.

MARIA EDGEWORTH

ROOFTOPS/*Belfast*

108

SCHOOL PATROLMAN WITH CHILDREN/*Belfast*

Take time to thrive, my ray of hope,
In the garden of Dromore.
Take heed, young eaglet, till thy wings
Are feathered fit to soar.
A little rest and then the world
Is full of work to do.
Sing hushaby loo, la loo, lolan,
Sing hushaby loo la loo.

ANCIENT FOLK SONG
"The Castle of Dromore"

THE COASTLINE
SEA AND ISLANDS

114

There are three islands:
Aranmor, the north island, about nine miles long;
Inishmaan, the middle island, about three miles and a half across,
and nearly round in form; and the south island, Inishere—
in Irish, east island —like the middle island but slightly smaller.
They lie about thirty miles from Galway, up the centre of the bay,
but they are not far from the cliffs of County Clare,
on the south, or the corner of Connemara on the north.

J. M. SYNGE
The Aran Islands

GRANDMOTHER WITH CHILDREN/*The Aran Islands*

There is a distant isle, around which sea-horses glisten,
a fair course on which the white wave surges,
four pedestals uphold it . . .

Unknown is wailing or treachery in the happy familiar land;
no sound there rough or harsh,
only sweet music striking on the ear . . .
There, there is neither "mine" nor "thine";
white are teeth there, dark the brows . . .
a wondrous land is the land I tell of,
youth does not give way to age there.

ANCIENT POEM
"The Voyage of Bran"

APPROACHING STORM/*Churchtown*

116

A man who is not afraid of the sea
will soon be drowned, he said,
for he will be going out on a day he shouldn't.
But we do be afraid of the sea,
and we do only be drowned now and again.

J. M. SYNGE
The Aran Islands

MEN PLAYING CARDS IN FRONT OF PUB/*County Kerry*

BOAT DOCK/*Duncannon*

MAN WITH PIPE/*Duncannon*

121

(OVERLEAF)
WALKING ON THE BEACH/*Dingle*

Gordon Wetmore
© 1980

CURRACHS

These long, light canoe-style boats of tarred canvas
stretched over laths are more seaworthy than they look.
They have been used by the island fishing fleets for centuries and
are remarkably agile: propelled by three experienced sets of
tapered oars, they can race through the water with the
speed and elegance of a shark, yet are sufficiently sturdy to
withstand the struggles of cattle being towed ashore.
This is a rather grisly operation, for the only method of
embarking any sizeable livestock for the two smaller islands is
to winch them down over the side of the mailboat into the water;
the head of the animal is then held firmly against the stern of
the *currach* and willy or nilly the rest of the beast swims along behind.

THORNTON COX
Travellers' Guide to Ireland

MAKING A CURRACH/*The Aran Islands*

MEN ROWING CURRACH/*Galway Bay*

Gordon Wetmore

© 1980

126

He passed unchallenged among the docks
and along the quays....
The vastness and strangeness
of the life suggested to him
by the bales of merchandise stocked
along the walls or swung aloft
out of the holds of steamers wakened again in him
the unrest which had sent him
wandering in the evening from garden to garden
in search of Mercedes.
And amid this new bustling life...
a vague dissatisfaction grew up within him
as he looked on the quays and on the river....

JAMES JOYCE
Portrait of an Artist as a Young Man

EARLY MORNING/*Waterford*

YOUNG GIRL/*Tralee*

Sweet is the voice in the land of gold,
And sweeter the music of birds that soar,
When the cry of the heron is heard on the Wold,
And the waves break softly on Bundatrore.

Down floats on the murmuring of the breeze
The call of the cuckoo from Cossahun,
The blackbird is warbling amongst the trees,
And soft is the kiss of the warming sun.

The cry of the eagle at Assaroe
O'er the court of MacMorne to me is sweet;
And sweet is the cry of the bird below,
Where the wave and the wind and the tall cliff meet.

Ancient Poem translated by Dean MacGregor

CHILDREN PLAYING ON BEACH/*Rosslare*

THE COUNTRYSIDE
PASTURES AND CASTLES

With deep affection,
And recollection,
I often think of
            Those Shandon bells,
Whose sounds so wild would,
In the days of childhood,
Fling around my cradle
            Their magic spells.
On this I ponder
Where'er I wander,
            And thus grow fonder,
Sweet Cork, of thee;
With thy bells of Shandon,
That sound so grand on
            The pleasant waters of the River Lee.

FRANCIS SYLVESTER MAHONY
"Father Prout"

FEEDING TIME/*County Tipperary*

An Englishman sets up an English home wherever he goes.
An Irishman takes root in the soil of his own country.
Even if he makes a home in another it has a real permanence.
His dream is always to come back.

KATHERINE T. HINKSON
"A Union of Hearts"

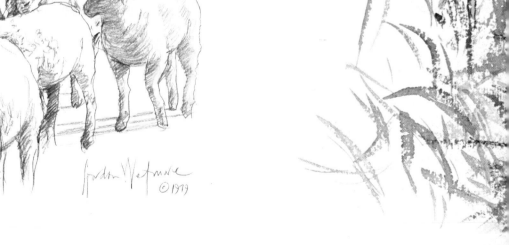

GIRLS HERDING SHEEP/*County Tipperary*

CHILDREN WITH GOAT/*River Barrow*

GUEST HOUSE/*Foulksmills*

I found in Munster unfettered of any,
Kings, and Queens, and poets a many—
Poets well skilled in music and measure,
Prosperous doings, mirth, and pleasure.

I found in Connaught the just, redundance
Of riches, milk in lavish abundance;
Hospitality, vigour, fame,
In Cruachan's land of heroic name.

I found in Ulster, from glen to glen,
Hardy warriors, resolute men;
Beauty that bloomed when youth was gone,
And strength transmitted from sire to son.

I found in Leinster the smooth and sleek,
From Dublin to Slewmargy's peak;
Flourishing pastures, valour, health,
Long-living worthies, commerce, wealth.

Translated by James Clarence Mangan from the twelfth-century Irish
"Prince Alfrid of Northumbria's Itinerary Through Ireland"

BRENNAN FARM/*Glen of Aherlow*

The splendour falls on castle walls
    And snowy summits old in story:
The long light shakes across the lakes,
    And the wild cataract leaps in glory.
Blow bugle, blow, set the wild echoes flying.
Blow, bugle; answer, echoes, dying, dying, dying.

O hark, O hear! how thin and clear,
    And thinner, clearer, farther going!
O sweet and far from cliff and scar
    The horns of Elfland faintly blowing!
Blow, let us hear the purple glens replying:
Blow, bugle; answer, echoes, dying, dying,
    dying...

ALFRED LORD TENNYSON
"The Princess"

CASTLE RUINS/County Kilkenny

Everything about Ireland,
her mountains, her streams,
her clouds and mist, her dew and sunshine,
her music that is the expansion of them all,
is made for allurement, especially for
the allurement of her conquerors.

KATHERINE T. HINKSON
"The Adventures of Alicia"

OLD FARMHOUSE/*Holy Cross*

141

HORSE RACES/*Thurles*

I met with Napper Tandy,
　　And he took me by the hand,
Saying, How is poor old Ireland,
　　And what way does she stand?
She's the most distressful country
　　That ever yet was seen;
They are hanging men and women
　　For the wearing of the green.

I care not for the Thistle,
　　And I care not for the Rose;
When bleak winds round us whistle,
　　Neither down nor crimson shows,
But like hope to him that's friendless,
　　When no joy around is seen,
O'er our graves with love that's endless
　　Blooms our own immortal green.

EIGHTEENTH-CENTURY SONG

RIDING LESSONS/*Holy Cross*

POINT TO POINT/*Thurles*

143

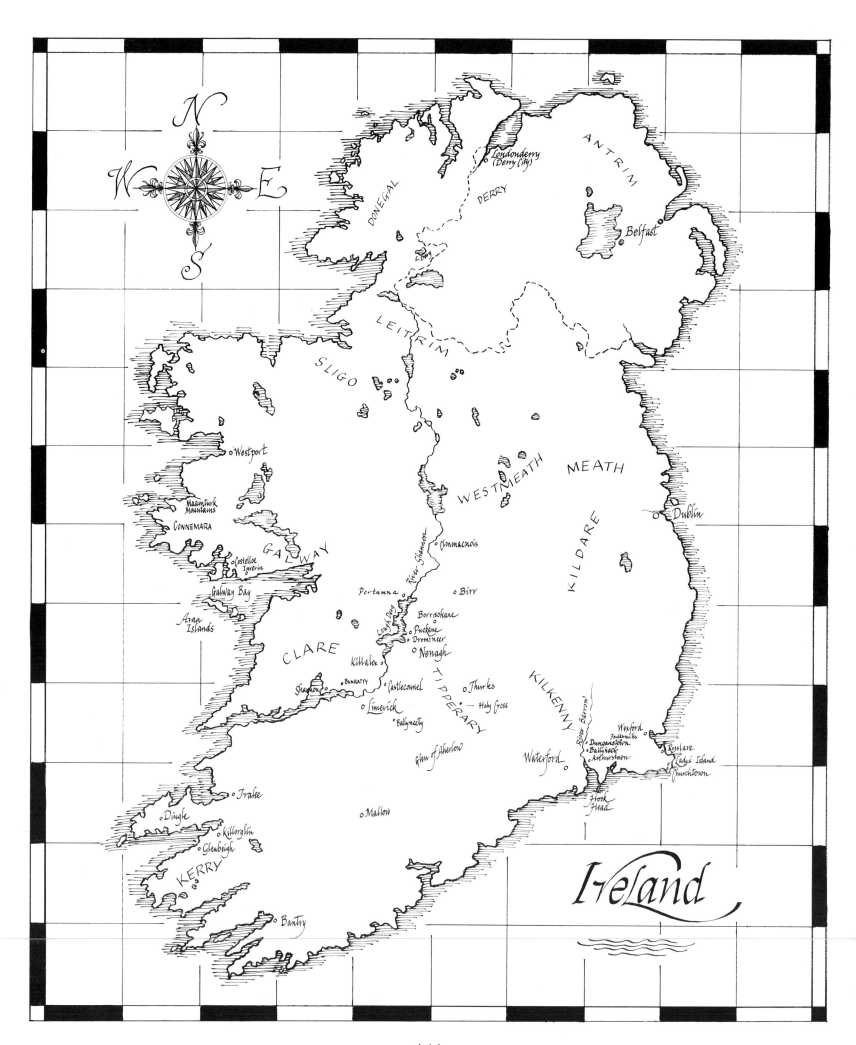